antipasti

antipasti

clare ferguson

photography by peter cassidy

RYLAND
PETERS
& SMALL
LONDON NEW YORK

For my husband, Ian Ferguson

First published in the United States in 2002
by Ryland Peters & Small, Inc.
519 Broadway, 5th Floor
New York, NY 10012
www.rylandpeters.com

10 9 8 7 6 5 4 3 2 1

Library of Congress Cataloging-in-Publication Data

Ferguson, Clare
    Antipasti : delicious Italian appetizers / by Clare Ferguson.
        p. cm
    ISBN 1-84172-254-5
    1. Appetizers. 2. Cookery, Italian. I. Title.

    TX740 .F467 2002
    641.8'12'0945--dc21   2001048829

Printed and bound in China

Designer	Luis Peral-Aranda
Commissioning Editor	Elsa Petersen-Schepelern
Production	Patricia Harrington
Art Director	Gabriella Le Grazie
Publishing Director	Alison Starling
Food Stylist	Clare Ferguson
Stylist	Antonia Gaunt

Notes

All spoon measurements used in this book are level.
Uncooked or partially cooked eggs should not be served to the very old or
frail, the very young, or pregnant women.
Ovens should be preheated to the specified temperature. Recipes in this
book were tested with a regular oven. If using a convection oven, decrease
the oven temperature by 40°F, or follow the manufacturer's instructions.

Sterilization of Preserving Jars

Wash the jars in hot, soapy water and rinse in boiling water. Place in a large
saucepan and then cover with hot water. With the lid on, bring the water to a
boil and continue boiling for 15 minutes. Turn off the heat, then leave the jars
in the hot water until just before they are to be filled. Invert the jars onto a
clean paper towel to dry. Sterilize the lids for 5 minutes, by boiling, or
according to the manufacturer's instructions. Jars should be filled and sealed
while they are still hot.

contents

an Italian introduction ...

Antipasti means "before the meal" in Italian—and these little dishes are some of the easiest, most tempting, delicious, and good-looking foods ever invented. It is no surprise that people all over the world love to eat antipasti at home, as well as in restaurants.

Many antipasti dishes are very simple, very stylish. For every Italian, they are the precursor to a good meal—a celebration of flavor, freshness, vitality, and fun. In Italy, a meal is seen as a whole, not a succession of dishes. Flavors, colors, textures are all equally harmonious: balance is important.

There are Italian trattorias and restaurants all over the globe that have long tables with big, beautiful displays of superb antipasti, so the diners are able to choose their own combination of dishes. However, at home, antipasti are often dishes bought ready-prepared, delicious, and handsome from a nearby gourmet store or specialist grocer. They are sometimes served on individual plates, but more often you help yourself from a large communal platter which is passed around the table. Please yourself: this is an informal way of eating. Three or four antipasti, some hot, some cold, if served together, can create a superb, very relaxed meal for family and friends.

Enjoy these antipasti: serve them with pride and pleasure and feel at peace with the world—Italians call it *allegria*—a sense of happiness. I cannot imagine anything better.

strong **flavors**, bright **colors**—
antipasti is the vibrant **soul**
of Italian food

cold dishes for hot days

Simple perfection: one of the most classic of all antipasti is this combination of fresh figs and prosciutto. Prosciutto crudo, with its distinctive silken, sweet-salt taste, is the excellent Italian cured, air-dried raw ham, sliced very thinly. The finest is San Daniele from Friuli, where the hams are slightly smaller than those from Parma. Aficionados consider the taste to be outstanding. If unavailable, try speck (cured smoked ham shoulder) or another salami (Italian preserved meat products) such as, say, mortadella. The combination of scented, soft fruit with elegant, mellow meat is bliss.

prosciutto crudo
with fresh figs

4–8 fresh, ripe figs, depending on size, halved or whole

8 slices prosciutto crudo, about 2 oz. per serving

freshly ground black pepper

grissini (Italian breadsticks) or Italian-style bread, to serve (optional)

Serves 4

Put the figs onto 4 plates. Add the slices of prosciutto arranged in loops or folds. Add freshly ground black pepper just before serving with grissini or crusty Italian bread.

Note Try to buy prosciutto from a specialist Italian food store or supermarket where you can ask for the slices to be cut thinly from a whole ham. Well sliced and laid out flat, you should be able to see through it. If buying packs of pre-cut ham, look for the designated label of origin: San Daniele and prosciutto di Parma are the ideal.

bresaola and arugula
with olive oil, and parmesan

Bresaola is Italian cured, air-dried beef—flavorful, deep crimson, lean, and succulent. Preferably it should be cut from a piece, sliced very thinly, but it is also available presliced, in packages. This combination of mellow, salty meat with the sharp, savory taste of Parmesan and high-quality extra virgin olive oil is simple, but wonderful.

12–16 thin slices of bresaola

2 oz. Parmesan cheese, in a piece

a large handful of arugula, torn

4–6 teaspoons high-quality extra virgin olive oil

Serves 4

Arrange the slices of bresaola on 4 serving plates.

Using a swivel-bladed vegetable peeler or sharp knife, shave off thin curls of the cheese and drop them on top of the bresaola.

Add the arugula, then drizzle with extra virgin olive oil and serve immediately.

marinated anchovies

Tiny, firm, white and silvery fillets of Italian marinated anchovies are sold packaged in jars or plastic packs. These have been prepared, filleted, and set in lemon or vinegar, or both. They can be eaten straight out of the jar, but taste even better with this easy, two-minute treatment.

Put the anchovy fillets onto a plate covered with paper towels. Pat the fillets dry with the towels, then separate them carefully. Transfer to a platter or 4 serving plates.

Drizzle the lemon juice over the top, then the olive oil. Arrange the onion on top of the anchovies, then sprinkle with chopped parsley, if using. They can also be served on bread or toast.

Note There are two kinds of bottled anchovies available. One is pinkish brown and salted, the other silver white and marinated. The second variety is the one used for this dish.

3–4 oz. bottled marinated anchovy fillets, drained

freshly squeezed juice of 1 lemon

1–2 tablespoons extra virgin olive oil

1 red onion, finely sliced into thin rounds

1 tablespoon finely chopped fresh flat-leaf parsley, to serve (optional)

Serves 4

cured tuna with lemon

In southern Italy, the tuna is outstanding. For this dish, choose belly tuna, the dense, red part of the fish. This keeps its fascinating texture when marinated and effectively "cooked" in the lemon juice, a little like the South American *ceviche*.

Slice the tuna into very fine slices using a fork and a very sharp knife.

Arrange the tuna in a single layer, in a non-metal, shallow dish. Sprinkle with the salt, sugar, and pepper. Cover and refrigerate for 5 minutes.

Pour over the lemon juice, then return the tuna to the refrigerator to chill until it becomes pale, opaque, and firm to the touch, almost as if cooked. This will take at least 5–10 minutes. (Refrigerate overnight if this is more convenient.)

To serve, drain off and discard most of the liquid. Transfer to a serving platter and top with the sliced scallions. Drizzle with olive oil, if using, then serve.

10 oz. belly tuna in a square or rectangular chunk

¼ cup salt flakes, preferably sea salt

4 teaspoons sugar

2 teaspoons coarsely crushed black peppercorns or hot red pepper flakes

½ cup freshly squeezed lemon juice, about 3–4 lemons

4 scallions, finely sliced

3–4 tablespoons extra virgin olive oil (optional)

Serves 4–6

shrimp with parsley and lemon

Shrimp are a very popular component of mixed seafood antipasti. Some shrimp are striped gray or blue; others have pearly, silvery shells or look almost translucent. This recipe suits almost any variety of shrimp—simply adjust the cooking time slightly to suit. Tails alone cook more quickly than whole shrimp and you also get more for the same weight.

1¾ lb. large, unpeeled shrimp, washed

2 tablespoons sea salt

1 tablespoon red wine vinegar

4 large sprigs of flat-leaf parsley, leaves reserved and chopped, stalks chopped finely

freshly squeezed juice of 2 lemons, plus 2 lemons, halved, to serve (optional)

2 tablespoons extra virgin olive oil

Serves 4

To devein the shrimp, cut a slit down the back into the flesh. Discard any black thread. Put 1 cup of water into a saucepan, add the salt, and bring to a boil. Add the shrimp and stir in the vinegar and parsley stalks. Return to a boil, reduce the heat, and cook gently for about 2–4 minutes, stirring and repositioning the shrimp now and then, until their flesh turns dense, white, and firm. The shells may change color, often to pink or scarlet.

Remove the cooked shrimp to a serving dish. Reserve 2 tablespoons of the cooking liquid and put into a small pitcher. Add the lemon juice, oil, and parsley leaves, mix well, then pour over the shrimp. Cool, then marinate them in the refrigerator for 10–20 minutes.

Serve with the lemon halves, paper napkins, finger bowls, and containers for the discarded shells.

Vitello tonnato is the famous dish of cold poached veal blanketed by a fascinating tuna-based sauce. The same idea can be used for eggplant. It is lushly delicious and pretty, too.

la tonnata di melanzane

1 large eggplant, about 12 oz.–1 lb.

3 tablespoons extra virgin olive oil

freshly cracked black pepper and salt

Tonnata sauce

4 oz. high-quality canned albacore tuna, packed in water, drained

2 tablespoons red or white wine vinegar

¼ cup capers, washed

2 teaspoons sun-dried tomato purée

⅓ cup mayonnaise

8 canned anchovies, washed, dried, and halved lengthwise

12 dry-cured black olives

Serves 4–6

Preheat the broiler, stove-top grill pan, or outdoor grill until hot.

Cut the eggplant crosswise into ¼-inch slices and brush one side with the oil. Cook the eggplant until tender and soft. When cooked, transfer to a serving plate, arranging the slices in overlapping rows.

Put 3 oz. of the drained tuna into a blender. Add the vinegar, capers, sun-dried tomato purée, and mayonnaise, and blend to a purée. Drizzle in enough ice water to make a thick, creamy, but pourable sauce.

Spoon the sauce over the eggplant, then add the remaining tuna, the anchovy slivers, and the olives.

Serve, sprinkled with salt and cracked black pepper.

Both of these olive recipes will keep well in a cool, dark place for weeks—or even months, if they get the chance. *Sott'olio* means "under oil."

black olives sott'olio

Put the coriander seeds, peppercorns, and garlic into a dry skillet and cook over a gentle heat, shaking and toasting until aromatic: do not let them scorch. Stir in the olives and cook for 2–3 minutes. Put the hot, sterilized jars onto a folded cloth or wooden board and, using a sterilized spoon, transfer the mixture into the jar(s). Push the lemon zest into the jar(s) using sterilized metal tongs.

Put the oil into a saucepan and heat to 350°F or until a small cube of bread turns golden brown in 40 seconds. Let cool for 2 minutes, then pour the oil carefully into the jar(s) until covered. Let cool, uncovered, and undisturbed. Top up with any unused oil, cover, and seal tightly. Store in a cool, dark cupboard until ready to serve.

Note Don't discard the oil—use it later for cooking.

¼ **cup coriander seeds, crushed**

2 **tablespoons black peppercorns**

8 **garlic cloves, halved lengthwise**

5 **cups imported black olives in brine, drained, patted dry, and pricked with a fork or sharp knife**

zest of 1 large, unwaxed lemon, removed in long strips

3 **cups extra virgin olive oil**

1½-quart jar or 3 pint jars, sterilized (page 4)

Makes 1 large or 3 small jars

If you have fennel flowers growing in your garden, use the whole seed heads for this dish. Otherwise, use fennel seeds.

green olives with fennel

3 cups imported preserved green olives, washed and dried with paper towels, then pricked with a fork

2 cups extra virgin olive oil

2 whole heads of fresh garlic, halved crosswise

4–8 fresh fennel flower heads, seeds intact (optional)

3 tablespoons black peppercorns, cracked or coarsely crushed

2 tablespoons fennel seeds

1 teaspoon cloves

1 quart jar or 2 pint jars, sterilized (page 4)

Makes 1 large or 2 small jars

Pack the olives loosely into the jar(s) with tongs or a spoon, but not your fingers.

Put the oil into a heavy saucepan and heat to 350°F or until a small cube of bread turns golden brown in about 40 seconds.

Using a slotted spoon, lower the halved garlic heads and the fennel flower heads into the oil. Let them sizzle briefly, for about 30 seconds, then lift them out and divide evenly between the jar(s). Scatter in the peppercorns, fennel seeds, and cloves. Top up with the remaining olives.

Pour the sizzling hot oil carefully over the olives until covered. Let cool for about 2 minutes, then pour the remaining oil carefully into the jar(s) until completely filled. Let cool, uncovered, and undisturbed. Seal tightly and store in a cool, dark cupboard until ready to serve.

parmesan wafers

Amazingly easy, delicious, and fun, these delicious wafers have many uses in the kitchen. Make more than the three or four per person you would allow for antipasti and keep the extras in an airtight container for snacks later, then briefly rebake them for absolute crispness, about five minutes or so.

If grating the cheese in a food processor, cut off and discard the hard, inedible rind. If grating by hand, leave it on to make the piece easier to hold.

Preheat the oven to 350°F and put the oven shelves toward the top of the oven.

Grate the cheese finely, then measure it out into piles of about 2 level tablespoons per pile.

Put 5 small piles of grated cheese onto each baking sheet and spread with a spoon to about 3–4 inches diameter. Bake each sheet in the preheated oven for 8–10 minutes or until golden, crisp, and frizzled, with bubbles all over: the cheese fuses together, miraculously.

Remove the hot wafers with a metal spatula. Let cool, flat, on a wire tray or curl them over a rolling pin or similar surface. Continue to cook and cool the remaining Parmesan wafers in the same way.

Note Never even consider using inferior, pregrated, so-called "Parmesan" for this or any other recipe: it is a travesty.

½ **lb. Parmesan cheese, in one piece**

4 baking sheets, preferably nonstick, brushed with oil or lined with wax paper

Serves 4–5: Makes 20

caponata

When I asked the photographer of this cookbook, Peter Cassidy, to name his favorite antipasto, he nominated caponata. This is no surprise, because his wife, Maria, is Sicilian and they make this dish superbly there.

1 eggplant, about 10 oz., cut into ½-inch cubes

1 tablespoon salt

¼ cup extra virgin olive oil

2 red onions, cut into 8 wedges each

4 garlic cloves, chopped

1 cup imported dry-cured green olives

¾ cup imported dry-cured black olives

⅓ cup capers in salt

2 teaspoons freshly chopped oregano or thyme leaves, plus extra sprigs, to serve (optional)

3 tomatoes, about 10 oz. total, cut into 8 wedges each

2 baby zucchini, about ½ lb., sliced crosswise

2 tablespoons tomato purée

2 teaspoons sugar

⅔ cup chicken or vegetable stock or water

¼ cup chopped, fresh flat-leaf parsley

Serves 6–8

Sprinkle the eggplant with the salt, toss well, and let stand for 10 minutes. Drain and pat dry with paper towels.

Put the oil into a large, heavy saucepan and heat until very hot. Add the onion, garlic, olives, and capers. Stir over high heat for 2–3 minutes, then add the eggplant and continue to cook, stirring, over medium heat for another 8 minutes. Using a slotted spoon, transfer the mixture to a plate and set aside.

Add the oregano, marjoram, or thyme to the pan, then add the tomatoes, zucchini, tomato purée, sugar, and stock or water. Stir gently and bring to a boil. Reduce the heat and simmer for 8 minutes. Return the eggplant mixture to the pan and simmer gently until the flavors have mingled. The vegetables should still be intact, not mushy.

Dip the pan into a bowl of cold water to cool.

To serve, transfer to a bowl, sprinkle with parsley, and top with the extra sprigs of oregano, marjoram, or thyme, if using. Caponata may be served warm, cool, or cold, but not chilled.

bread and salads

Mozzarella in carozza means "mozzarella in a carriage"—a romantic idea when you think of the handsome horse-drawn carriages seen in many Italian cities. They are, essentially, bread and cheese sandwiches, egg-dipped, and fried to a luscious, oozy crispness. (Another version of this classic dish is made using sliced eggplant.) Rich though they are, they taste blissful.

mozzarella in carozza

4 large slices of coarse, country-style Italian bread, such as Puglièse

¼ lb. mozzarella cheese, finely sliced

8 canned anchovy fillets or salt, to taste

½ cup milk

2 eggs

freshly ground black pepper (optional)

virgin olive oil, for frying

Serves 2 or 4

Put the slices of bread onto a board. Arrange the sliced mozzarella over 2 of the slices and put the anchovies, if using, on top. Season with pepper (not salt, if using anchovies, which are salty). Put the other slices of bread on top.

Put the milk and eggs into a shallow dish and beat well.

Pour about 1 inch depth of the virgin olive oil into a large, heavy skillet. Heat to 375°F or until a small cube of bread turns golden brown in about 40 seconds. Have a spatula or slotted spoon ready.

Dip the sandwiches into the egg mixture until thoroughly wet.

Using the spatula or slotted spoon, slide both sandwiches into the hot oil and fry for about 4–5 minutes, turning them over carefully, once, using tongs.

Remove from the oil with the tongs or a slotted spoon, then drain on paper towels. Serve whole or sliced into pieces and eat them hot.

toasted focaccia
with borlotti beans and greens

Good, toasted bread, with a coarse mash of beans on top and a handful of wild salad leaves, is a country treat. If you don't have time to soak and cook the dried cranberry beans from scratch, of course you can use canned beans. The greens shown here are baby dandelion leaves. Good vegetable markets sometimes have them or, if you have a yard, you probably have them as weeds (use only the youngest leaves). Other greens such as frisée, arugula, or watercress could be substituted if necessary.

4 slices focaccia, sliced about ¾ inch thick

2 garlic cloves, crushed

¼ cup extra virgin olive oil

14 oz. canned cranberry beans*

1 teaspoon sea salt flakes

1 teaspoon freshly ground black pepper

2 handfuls of fresh dandelion leaves or other bitter salad greens

freshly squeezed juice of 1 lemon

Serves 4

Toast the bread on both sides, preferably on a preheated stove-top grill pan or outdoor grill. While still hot, rub the toast on one side with a crushed garlic clove and drizzle with half the oil. Keep hot.

Put the remaining oil into a saucepan and heat gently. Add the remaining garlic and sauté briefly until aromatic but not brown. Add the drained beans and mash coarsely with a fork. Add the salt and pepper and cook, stirring, until heated through.

Put the hot toast onto 4 serving plates, spoon the bean mixture on top, then add a pile of leaves. Sprinkle with lemon juice and serve while the toast is warm, the beans hot, and the salad still bouncy.

To serve as party food, cut small squares of bread to make tiny versions of this dish.

*Note If you are using dried beans, use 1 cup. Soak them overnight in cold water to cover, then drain. Put into a large saucepan, cover with boiling water, and return to a boil. Reduce the heat and simmer until done, about 1½–2 hours, depending on the age of the beans.

squid with gremolata
on toasted country bread

Squid perfectly suits this untraditional topping of garlic, lemon, and parsley with optional cheese—a garnish usually reserved for the classic Italian dish *osso buco*. Make sure that the toast is warm and the squid is dry and well coated before it is fried.

First, toast the bread on one side only.

To make the gremolata, put the lemon zest, parsley, and garlic into a bowl and toss lightly. Keep it light, not dense. Add the grated cheese, if using, and toss.

Slice the squid bodies crosswise into ½-inch rings. Put the cornmeal, polenta, or flour and salt into a bowl, add the squid rings and tentacles, if any, and toss to coat.

Pour about ½ inch depth of the olive oil into a heavy saucepan. Heat to 375°F or until a small cube of bread turns golden brown in about 40 seconds. Add the prepared squid in 2–3 batches and cook for 1–1½ minutes at the most: too much heat and the squid will become tough. Remove with a slotted spoon and transfer to a plate lined with paper towels. Keep each batch hot in the oven while you cook the remainder.

Pile the squid on top of the toasts, sprinkle with the gremolata, then serve.

Note If you have to clean the squid yourself, it's very easy and not at all messy. Pull the tentacles out of the bodies. Trim off and discard the eyes and tiny hard beak in the middle of the star of tentacles. Rinse out the contents of the body and discard the transparent quill. Although the pinky mauve skin is often rubbed off and removed from the squid, I think it looks and tastes better if left on.

1 small loaf of Italian-style bread, thickly sliced, or 1 ciabatta loaf, halved lengthwise, then crosswise

Gremolata

finely shredded zest of 1 lemon

a large bunch of flat-leaf parsley, coarsely chopped, about ¼ oz.

4 garlic cloves, crushed and finely chopped

¼ cup freshly grated Parmesan cheese (optional)

Squid

1¼ lb. prepared squid, about 8–10 inches long, or 10 oz. prepared squid rings

¾ cup fine cornmeal, polenta, or all-purpose flour

1 teaspoon coarse salt

virgin olive oil, for frying

Serves 4

This homemade black olive paste is pungently delicious:
a perfect antipasto to keep on hand. It is served with a
regional flatbread from Sardinia, *carta da musica* (it
looks like fine sheets of paper), which is often dried
into crisp, brittle round sheets. The bread is exported in
hard cardboard boxes to protect it from damage.

hot flatbreads with black olive paste

6–8 sheets *carta da musica* or grissini (Italian breadsticks)

1–2 tablespoons extra virgin olive oil

Black olive paste

3 cups imported dry-cured black olives

2 tablespoons capers, rinsed

8 canned anchovy fillets, rinsed and chopped

½ teaspoon freshly ground black pepper

1 small, hot chile pepper, finely chopped, or 1 garlic clove, chopped (optional)

1 teaspoon dried oregano, marjoram, or thyme

⅓ cup extra virgin olive oil

Serves 4–6

Brush one side of the bread with the first measure of olive oil. Transfer to a preheated oven and bake at 400°F for 8–10 minutes, then turn off the oven and leave the door slightly ajar.

To make the paste, pit the olives. Put the olives into a food processor, then add the capers, anchovies, pepper, chile or garlic, and oregano, marjoram, or thyme. Chop in several short, pulsing bursts. With the machine running, slowly pour in the oil through the feed tube, until the mixture forms a rich, coarse purée. Don't overprocess: some contrast in texture is important.

Serve the olive paste with the hot, crisp flatbreads. The paste may be stored in the refrigerator for up to 2 weeks.

panzanella

A great antipasto for summer or fall, this Tuscan dish has been adapted and interpreted worldwide. It depends upon superb, ripe, flavorful ingredients, so make it whenever you find you have wonderful sweet peppers, tomatoes, and fresh, bouncy basil leaves.

3–4 thick slices crusty country bread, torn into pieces

2 red bell peppers

2 yellow bell peppers

3 medium, ripe, juicy tomatoes

3–4 garlic cloves, crushed to a purée

⅓–½ cup extra virgin olive oil

1 tablespoon red wine vinegar

2 teaspoons balsamic vinegar

6 anchovy fillets, halved lengthwise

6 caperberries or 2 tablespoons salted capers

a small bunch of basil

a few celery leaves (optional)

Serves 4–6

Cut or pull the bread into 1-inch chunks or smaller, and either leave plain or toast briefly under a preheated broiler or on a grill.

To prepare the red and yellow bell peppers, cut them into quarters, and cook under a hot broiler until the skins blister. Remove the skins and reserve the flesh. To prepare the tomatoes, dip into a pan of boiling water for about 30 seconds, then remove and pull off the skins. Put the tomatoes into a strainer set over a bowl to catch the juices. Cut or tear the tomatoes in half, then remove and discard the seeds.

Cut or tear the tomatoes into smaller pieces and put into the bowl of juice. Add the garlic, oil, and two vinegars, and stir to make a dressing.

Put the anchovies and caperberries or capers into a bowl, cover with boiling water, let soak for 5 minutes, then drain.

Put the bread, tomatoes, peppers, caperberries or capers, anchovies, and half the basil into a bowl. Pour over the dressing and enough of the caper-anchovy soaking liquid to give a good flavor.

Toss gently and let stand for 10–20 minutes. Top with the reserved basil and celery leaves, if using, then serve.

verdure in pinzimonio
crudités with extra virgin olive oil

⅔ cup high quality extra virgin olive oil

salt and freshly cracked black pepper

Your choice of:

8 baby carrots

8 radishes or baby turnips, with green tops

2 small fennel bulbs, trimmed and cut into 8 wedges each

2 celery hearts, trimmed and quartered lengthwise

2 baby artichokes, halved lengthwise

a small bunch of baby asparagus

8 scallions, trimmed

1 red or yellow bell pepper, cut into 8 wedges and seeded

Serves 4

This is the Italian version of crudités with vinaigrette. Choose the crispest baby vegetables you can find, plus a few herbs, then serve them with the best extra virgin olive oil. Some vegetables, such as baby artichokes, may have to be parboiled, then refreshed in ice water before serving.

Put a layer of ice cubes into a serving bowl, add 1 cup water, then pack the vegetables on top. Put the olive oil into 4 small bowls and the salt and pepper into grinders or tiny bowls. Provide plenty of paper napkins.

To eat, take a piece of vegetable out of the bowl, dry it on a paper napkin, dip into the oil, then into salt and pepper.

Radicchio, the bitter red Italian chicory, is used as a salad leaf and also cooked as a vegetable. The round-headed Verona variety is available all year round, while Treviso, the version with long leaves, is usually only available during fall and winter. If you can't find them, use another bitter green, such as frisée or escarole, instead. Teamed with velvety blue Gorgonzola and walnuts, this is an utterly irresistible combination.

radicchio with gorgonzola and walnuts

4–5 oz. Gorgonzola cheese

1 head of radicchio

1 head of Treviso

2 tablespoons extra virgin olive oil (optional)

¾ cup shelled walnuts or pecans

freshly ground black pepper

Serves 4

Slice or break the cheese into 2-inch wedges or chunks.

Separate the radicchio and Treviso into leaves.

Arrange the leaves on small serving plates, drizzle with olive oil, if using, add the Gorgonzola, and walnuts or pecans, then serve, sprinkled with freshly ground black pepper.

In Italian markets, you see small boxes of different baby leaves, often wild. Shoppers choose a handful each of their favorite kinds to make a mixed salad. Originally, the mixture was picked from wild plants in the fields (*campo* means "field") and still is in country areas, so the mixture should include herbs, bitter leaves, soft greens, and crunchy leaves.

insalata di campo

¾ lb. wild leaves or herbs

1 tablespoon balsamic vinegar

⅓–½ cup extra virgin olive oil

freshly squeezed juice of ½ lemon

salt and freshly ground black pepper

2 oz. hard cheese, such as Parmesan, in one piece, to serve

Serves 4–6

Wash the leaves well in a large bowl of cold water. Drain and shake or spin them dry without crushing or bruising them. Transfer to a clean dishcloth lined with paper towels. Wrap the leaves in the dishcloth and refrigerate for about 30 minutes.

Put the vinegar, oil, lemon juice, salt, and pepper into a bowl and beat well to form a dressing.

Using a swivel-bladed vegetable peeler, remove fine, long, thin curls of cheese from the block, then set them aside.

When ready to serve, put the leaves into a salad bowl. Beat the dressing briefly and sprinkle over the salad. Toss gently until everything gleams, then top with the cheese shavings and serve.

Note Choose a combination of leaves—whatever is fresh and good on the day. Suggestions include arugula, young dandelion leaves, lamb's lettuce (mâche or corn salad), flat-leaf parsley, baby spinach, sprigs of dill, and nasturtium leaves.

½ cup unsalted butter, melted

6–8 garlic cloves,
crushed to a purée

⅓ cup extra virgin olive oil

4 oz. canned anchovy fillets,
drained, chopped, and mashed

Your choice of:

red, yellow, or orange bell
peppers (but not green), cut into
8 wedges and seeded

sweet banana peppers,
halved, cored, and seeded

celery stalks

Belgian endive

Treviso

inner leaves from
romaine lettuce

scallions

baby asparagus

cauliflower florets

broccoli florets, quartered
lengthwise

fennel bulbs,
cut into wedges lengthwise

sprigs of flat-leaf parsley

Serves 4–8

In some parts of Italy, this intensely flavorful dip is made with olive oil: in others, it is made with butter, particularly in the north. The two styles work equally well, but my own version combines both methods, and speeds the process wonderfully. Amazingly, the result is mellow and smooth, not aggressively pungent at all. The crisp, sweet, mild vegetables offset the salty flavor of the sauce.

bagna cauda

Put the butter and garlic into a nonstick skillet and heat gently, until the butter has melted. Transfer to a blender and add the olive oil and anchovies. Purée for 2–3 minutes, then transfer to a serving bowl. The bowl of dip should be kept hot over a low candle flame.

Surround the hot dip with the prepared cold, crisp vegetables.

Note The traditional method is to put the butter and puréed garlic into a shallow terracotta dish and stir for 5–10 minutes over low to medium heat. Add the anchovy fillets and mash over the heat. Add the oil, reheat gently, then serve as above.

hot vegetable antipasti

Peppers are ubiquitous ingredients in antipasti: they respond well to broiling and roasting, two methods that develop the natural sugars. Mixed with salty anchovies and sharp pickled caperberries or capers, they really come into their own. This recipe is from southern Italy—easy, elegant, and delicious.

peperoni farciti

4 red or yellow bell peppers, quartered lengthwise and seeded

16 canned anchovy fillets, rinsed and drained

16 caperberries or 2 tablespoons capers, rinsed and drained

a small bunch of marjoram or oregano, chopped

2 tablespoons extra virgin olive oil

freshly ground black pepper

Serves 4

Arrange the quartered peppers in a large roasting dish or pan.

Using kitchen shears or a small knife, cut each anchovy fillet lengthwise into 2 strips. Put 2 strips into each pepper segment. Add a caperberry or a share of the capers to each segment, and sprinkle with the chopped herbs and olive oil.

Roast, uncovered, toward the top of a preheated oven at 350°F for about 20–30 minutes or until wrinkled, aromatic, and beginning to char a little at the edges. Serve hot, warm, or cool, sprinkled with black pepper.

Note Use any color pepper other than green—green tastes too acidic.

deep-fried zucchini flowers

One of the most famous of Italian dishes, this celebrates springtime and sunshine, while the paradox of tender flowers in crunchy batter is a revelation. Zucchini flowers are a special seasonal treat—buy them whenever you see them in the market. They can also be stuffed with herbs and ricotta or breadcrumbs, then baked in the oven.

16–20 zucchini flowers

3 eggs, separated

¼ teaspoon salt

freshly ground black pepper

a pinch of powdered saffron (optional)

6 tablespoons light beer, preferably Italian

1 cup all-purpose flour, sifted

virgin olive oil, for deep-frying

sea salt flakes, to serve

Serves 4

Check the flowers for insects, but don't wash them. If the zucchini are still attached, slice them off and use for another dish.

Put the egg whites into a bowl and beat to a froth. Put the egg yolks into a second bowl, add the salt, pepper, saffron, if using, and 2 tablespoons of the beer. Fold in the sifted flour and remaining beer to make a light, foamy batter, then fold in the frothy egg whites.

Put the oil into a deep saucepan and heat to 375°F. Working in batches of 4–5, dip the flowers, stem end first, into the batter. Deep-fry in the hot oil for 2–3 minutes, until deep gold and delicately crisp. Remove with a slotted spoon or tongs. Drain on crumpled paper towel set on a wire rack, and keep hot while you fry the remainder.

Serve immediately, sprinkled with sea salt flakes: these need no accompaniment at all.

Note No flowers available? Use baby zucchini instead, slicing them into quarters, lengthwise.

crushed cannellini beans
with garlic, rosemary, and wilted greens

A wonderful peasant dish, satisfying and earthy. It is delicious served on small, oven-crisped pieces of bread, crackers, toasted focaccia, or ciabatta squares.

1 cup dried cannellini beans

1 tomato, crushed

8 sprigs of rosemary, crushed

4 garlic cloves, crushed

4–6 tablespoons extra virgin olive oil

1 tablespoon sea salt flakes

freshly ground pepper

¼–½ lb. broccoli rabe, chard, or spinach leaves

grilled ciabatta or other Italian bread, to serve (optional)

Serves 4–6

Put the dried beans into a bowl, cover with cold water, and let soak for 8–12 hours. Drain, then transfer to a large saucepan, cover with boiling water, and bring to a boil. Add the crushed tomato, half the rosemary, and half the garlic. Cook, part-covered, at a gentle simmer for 1½–1¾ hours or until the beans are tender (they will squash easily between the fingers).

Strain but reserve 1 ladle (about 1–1¼ cups) of the cooking liquid. Discard the rosemary, but reserve the cooked tomato and garlic.

Put half the olive oil into the still-hot, empty pan, then add the remaining garlic and rosemary. Stir in the beans, salt, and pepper. Using a potato masher or large fork, squash them slightly to a coarse mash. Mix in enough of the hot bean cooking liquid to produce a creamy texture.

Put the remaining oil in a separate pan, heat gently, then add the broccoli rabe, chard, or spinach. Sauté quickly until brilliantly green and wilted. Serve the beans topped with the greens, alone or on grilled bread, if using.

Delectable and easy, this antipasto is known and served all around the shores of the Mediterranean, with small local variations. Serve it plain or pile it up on crusty or toasted bread pieces, or even combine it with a little pasta, rice, or polenta for a more substantial appetizer.

spinach with pine nuts
garlic and anchovies

¼ **cup extra virgin olive oil, preferably Italian**

¼ **cup pine nuts**

8–10 anchovy fillets, salted or canned

4 garlic cloves, crushed

¼ **cup seedless dark raisins or golden raisins**

1½ **lb. well-washed spinach, water still clinging**

freshly ground black pepper

Serves 4–6

Put half the oil into a skillet, add the pine nuts, and cook over high heat, shaking the skillet and stirring often, until they turn golden all over. Remove the nuts with a slotted spoon and set aside.

Rinse the anchovies in warm water, drain, then chop coarsely. Add the garlic to the skillet, add the anchovies, and crush and mash them well over the heat.

Add the remaining oil, dark or golden raisins, and the still-wet spinach, chopped coarsely if the leaves are large. Toss carefully using tongs or a wooden spoon, until all the ingredients are evenly distributed. Cover the pan and cook over medium heat for about 2–3½ minutes, stirring halfway through.

Uncover the pan. Add the pine nuts and stir gently until evenly heated through. Serve hot or warm, sprinkled with pepper and with the pan juices trickled on top.

beans in "saor"
(sweet-sour marinade)

1¼ lb. green, yellow, or wax beans, stalk ends trimmed

1 carrot, sliced

¼ cup balsamic vinegar

salt

Marinade

¼ cup extra virgin olive oil

1 onion, sliced into rounds

1 tablespoon black peppercorns

4 fresh bay leaves, crushed

½ cup white wine vinegar

¼ cup dry white wine or water

2 tablespoons almonds, pine nuts, or hazelnuts

2 tablespoons capers

2 tablespoons clear honey or sugar (optional)

sea salt

Serves 6–8

This unusual treatment is often used for fish as well as vegetables. It is popular in the Veneto region and can be traced back centuries. However, the balsamic vinegar reduction is a new idea and is deliciously rich and sticky.

Bring a large saucepan of lightly salted water to a boil. Add the beans and carrots, cook gently for about 3–5 minutes, until *al dente* (cooked but crisp). Drain, cool quickly under cold running water, and drain again.

To make the marinade, put the oil into a saucepan and heat gently. Add the onion and sauté briefly until translucent. Stir in the peppercorns, bay leaves, vinegar, wine or water, nuts, capers, and honey or sugar, if using. Cook over a gentle heat for 4–5 minutes until the flavors have blended.

Add the beans and carrots, toss gently, then transfer to a bowl or plate and season to taste.

Put the balsamic vinegar into a small saucepan, bring to a boil, and simmer until reduced to half its volume. Drizzle or dot this sticky sauce over the beans and serve. (The vinegar gives a bittersweet caramel edge to the dish.)

Once, in a fruit and vegetable market in Rome, I saw a brawny stall-holder holding long-stemmed baby artichokes, heads down, squashed out flat like daisies, in hot olive oil. When crisp, they were transferred to a battered plate covered with torn paper and served to appreciative passers-by, to advertise the sweet baby artichokes on his stall. This recipe calls for tiny globe artichoke heads, preferably with violet petals and no more than two inches long. Try it: it is a fascinating recipe, perfect for spring.

deep-fried baby artichokes

10–12 tiny globe artichokes, preferably with stalks attached

virgin olive oil, for frying

To serve

lemon wedges

sea salt and freshly ground pepper

Serves 4–6

Cut the artichokes into quarters lengthwise.

Fill a saucepan with the olive oil to a depth of 2 inches. Heat to about 375°F or until a small cube of bread turns brown within 40 seconds.

Add the artichokes, 6–8 at a time and, using a slotted spoon, push them down hard against the bottom of the pan. Fry until they are crisp and smell caramelized. Carefully remove with tongs or a slotted spoon and drain, stems upward. Keep hot or warm while you cook the remainder.

Remove the stalks and serve the frizzled heads sprinkled with salt and pepper and with lemon wedges for squeezing.

pan-grilled eggplant
with pine nuts and garlic

Eggplant, known as *melanzane* in Italy, is a versatile vegetable, cherished all over the Mediterranean, all over the globe. Fresh ones should be glossy and firm to the touch. These days, new breeds have little of the traditional bitterness, so need no pre-salting. This is a quick, light, easy snack.

2 medium eggplant, about 1½ lb. total

⅓ cup extra virgin olive oil

1 cup pine nuts

a small bunch of fresh mint, half chopped, half in sprigs

4 garlic cloves, crushed (optional)

½–1 tablespoon sea salt

Serves 4

Slice the eggplant lengthwise into slices just under ½ inch thick, about 12–16 slices in total. Using a fork, score both sides of each slice several times in a crisscross pattern. Brush a little olive oil on both sides of the slices.

Preheat a stove-top grill pan or nonstick skillet until very hot. Drizzle with a few teaspoons of the remaining oil. Cook half the eggplant slices, pressing them down firmly, for about 3 minutes on each side or until tender and firmly griddle-marked. Remove from the pan, roll them up loosely, and keep them warm. Repeat with the remaining slices.

Add the pine nuts to the oiled, hot pan, and toast gently, stirring them about to prevent scorching. Set aside.

Finally, put the remaining olive oil into a bowl, add the chopped mint, garlic, if using, and sea salt, and mix to form a dressing.

Serve the eggplant drizzled with dressing and dotted with the remaining mint sprigs.

Variation Add sun-dried or semi-dried (sun-blushed) tomatoes and a little of their rosy oil.

hot seafood antipasti

Last time I was in Venice, I had delicious mussels from the Venetian lagoon, served in a tangle of fine, plain spaghetti. This recipe can be served plain, on garlic toasts, or combined with pasta, rice, or even a little polenta. It is delectably easy and good, whichever way you choose.

mussels
with garlic, parsley, and lemon

2 lb. large mussels, scrubbed

4 garlic cloves, chopped

2 tablespoons extra virgin olive oil

⅓ cup white wine

a long strip of zest and freshly squeezed juice of 1 lemon

a small bunch of fennel fronds or parsley, chopped

freshly ground black pepper

Serves 4

Pull off and discard the beards from the mussels. Tap any open mussels against the work surface: if they don't close immediately, discard them. Scrub the mussels briefly and rinse again.

Put the mussels into a heavy saucepan, add the garlic, oil, white wine, lemon zest, and juice, and bring to a boil. Cover, reduce the heat to medium, and cook, undisturbed, for 3–4 minutes or until the shells are open and the mussels plumply cooked (discard any mussels that don't open).

Add half the chopped fennel or parsley. Stir, then cover again for 1 minute. Remove and discard the empty half-shells from the mussels.

Transfer the mussels into 1 large or 4 small bowls or plates. Sprinkle the remaining parsley on top and add generous grinds of black pepper. Eat hot or warm, with crusty bread to mop up the delicious juices.

Variation Add 1 large tomato, cut into tiny cubes, and omit the lemon zest.

clams with chile parsley sauce

Clam dishes in Italy are wonderful and this sweet shellfish is used in many different ways, all simple and delicious. For instance, *pasta con le vongole*—pasta with clam sauce—is one of my favorites.

2 lb. littleneck clams, scrubbed, rinsed, and drained

¼ cup extra virgin olive oil

1 teaspoon hot red pepper flakes

4 garlic cloves, chopped

1 onion, finely chopped

½ cup dry or sweet white vermouth

freshly ground black pepper

a handful of parsley, chopped, plus 4–6 leaves, to serve (optional)

Serves 4–6

Put the clams, olive oil, pepper flakes, garlic, onion, vermouth, and black pepper into a large saucepan. Bring to a boil, cover tightly with a lid, reduce the heat, and let steam for about 4–6 minutes.

Stir in the chopped parsley and cover again. Turn off the heat, let steam for a further 1 minute, then serve, topped with a parsley leaf, if using.

Note Canned or bottled clams in the shell are available in Italian gourmet stores: useful if you can't find any fresh clams. If using them, drain the liquid into the pan, add all the remaining ingredients except the clams, bring to a boil, and reduce to about 1 cup. Add the drained clams, then steam just until the clams have been heated through. Serve as before.

sizzled scallops with lemon

Scallops are a popular seafood in Italy. Allow three or four scallops per person, depending on their size, your appetite, and your budget. If using frozen scallops, they must be fully thawed, patted dry, and cooked more carefully, because they absorb a lot of water and create more steam.

Put 1 teaspoon of the lemon zest into a bowl, add the sea salt and garlic, and mix gently.

Pat the scallops dry with paper towels and add to the bowl.

Heat a nonstick skillet, add the butter and olive oil, and heat until sizzling. Add the scallops and cook for 1–1½ minutes on each side or until golden. The inside should be barely heated through, barely cooked, silky smooth, and opaque.

Reduce the heat and add the lemon juice and wine or vermouth. Push the scallops to one side. Tilt the pan to pool the juices. Add the mascarpone or cream cheese, if using, and stir it into the sauce. Heat until the sauce thickens slightly and evaporates to a creamy glaze.

Serve the scallops inside the deep shells or on small plates with the sliced lemon and toasted ciabatta.

finely grated zest and freshly squeezed juice of 1 lemon

1 teaspoon salt

2 garlic cloves, crushed

12–16 prepared scallops, and their deep shells if available

4 tablespoons butter, melted

2 tablespoons extra virgin olive oil

2 tablespoons white wine or vermouth

2 tablespoons mascarpone or cream cheese, cut into small pieces (optional)

To serve

1 lemon, halved and sliced

sliced ciabatta bread, toasted

Serves 4–6

Calamaretti (baby squid) are a favorite in Italy, especially in seaside trattorias. If your fish seller doesn't have fresh baby squid, he will almost certainly have fresh or frozen prepared squid bodies. Buy the smallest you can find, fill them loosely, and cook for a few minutes more until firm and densely white. You will miss out on the crispy tentacles and the flavorful pink skins, but the dish will still taste good.

stuffed oven-roasted baby squid

1 lb. whole baby squid, fresh or frozen and thawed

½ teaspoon salt

¼ teaspoon hot red pepper flakes or crushed black peppercorns

¼–⅓ cup extra virgin olive oil, heated until very hot

Herb stuffing

2 tablespoons chopped fresh marjoram, oregano, or dill

¼ cup chopped fresh flat-leaf parsley

2 slices prosciutto or cooked ham, chopped

2 teaspoons grated fresh lemon zest

2 slices stale white bread, crumbled

Serves 4–6

To make the stuffing, put the herbs, prosciutto or ham, lemon zest, and bread into a food processor and chop in a series of brief pulses. The mixture should be coarse.

Wash and drain the squid and pat dry with paper towels. Pull the tentacles out of the bodies. Trim off and discard the eyes and tiny beak in the middle of the star of tentacles. Rinse out the contents of the body and discard the transparent quill. Some people remove the pinky mauve skin from the squid, but I think it adds flavor and color.

Loosely pack the stuffing mixture inside the squid bodies. Close the ends with a toothpick. Dust the stuffed squid and the tentacles with the salt and hot red pepper flakes or pepper. Arrange them in a shallow roasting pan.

Put the olive oil into a saucepan and heat until hot. Pour over the squid and roast toward the top of a preheated oven at 400°F for 5–8 minutes or until the flesh sets white and firm and the stuffing smells aromatic. Serve hot or warm.

index

conversion charts

Weights and measures have been rounded up or down slightly to make measuring easier.

Volume equivalents:

American	Metric	Imperial
1 teaspoon	5 ml	
1 tablespoon	15 ml	
¼ cup	60 ml	2 fl.oz.
⅓ cup	75 ml	2½ fl.oz.
½ cup	125 ml	4 fl.oz.
⅔ cup	150 ml	5 fl.oz. (¼ pint)
¾ cup	175 ml	6 fl.oz.
1 cup	250 ml	8 fl.oz.

Weight equivalents:

Measurements:

Imperial	Metric	Inches	Cm
1 oz.	25 g	¼ inch	5 mm
2 oz.	50 g	½ inch	1 cm
3 oz.	75 g	¾ inch	1.5 cm
4 oz.	125 g	1 inch	2.5 cm
5 oz.	150 g	2 inches	5 cm
6 oz.	175 g	3 inches	7 cm
7 oz.	200 g	4 inches	10 cm
8 oz. (½ lb.)	250 g	5 inches	12 cm
9 oz.	275 g	6 inches	15 cm
10 oz.	300 g	7 inches	18 cm
11 oz.	325 g	8 inches	20 cm
12 oz.	375 g	9 inches	23 cm
13 oz.	400 g	10 inches	25 cm
14 oz.	425 g	11 inches	28 cm
15 oz.	475 g	12 inches	30 cm
16 oz. (1 lb.)	500 g		
2 lb.	1 kg		

Oven temperatures:

110°C	(225°F)	Gas ¼
120°C	(250°F)	Gas ½
140°C	(275°F)	Gas 1
150°C	(300°F)	Gas 2
160°C	(325°F)	Gas 3
180°C	(350°F)	Gas 4
190°C	(375°F)	Gas 5
200°C	(400°F)	Gas 6
220°C	(425°F)	Gas 7
230°C	(450°F)	Gas 8
240°C	(475°F)	Gas 9